CARE
THE OLDER

CONTENTS

INTRODUCTION

HOW OLD IS OLD?

Time waits for no man and he is, unfortunately, less patient when it comes to our canine friends. With a bit of luck we can expect to be around well into our seventies, but our pets are only allowed to spend a relatively small proportion of that time with us. Like us they go through three life stages: growth, which takes from twelve to eighteen months, then adulthood, finally entering old age from nine years onwards. We often hear people say that every year in a dog's life is equivalent to seven human years, but it is not as simple as that. Generally speaking,

A German Shepherd in prime condition

Yorkshire Terrier aged thirteen years

small dogs live longer than large dogs, often into their teens. The life expectancy of an Irish Wolfhound or a Saint Bernard is as little as six years.

Thanks to better living conditions, an improved diet and superior health care, our quality of life and life expectancy are far superior to those of our ancestors. For similar reasons pets too are living longer but, as members of our family, our pets depend upon us to ensure that we take the necessary steps to ensure that they also have a long and happy life.

An old Beagle makes friends with a child

FEEDING

As dogs progress from puppyhood, through maturity to old age, their nutritional requirements alter. Puppies reach maturity at anything from twelve to twenty-four months, depending upon size, and they require relatively high levels of protein, carbohydrates and fat along with adequate levels of vitamins and minerals to ensure healthy growth. As mature adults those requirements change and they alter again as they enter their latter years.

Generally speaking, we need to monitor carefully the amount of protein, sodium, phosphate, saturated fat and calories we

A fifteen-year-old example of a breed not often seen – the Karabash

Many people now feed their dogs with one of the commercially prepared feeds

feed to our older pets and, in the majority of cases, this will mean a reduction in quantities. On the other hand, we will probably want to increase the level of vitamins, certain minerals and fibre. In specific individuals, for example in cases of diabetes mellitus, kidney failure or bladder stones, special dietary requirements may be indicated. Although, in theory, it may be possible to formulate a home-made diet suitable for an elderly dog, it is easier and better for all concerned to use one of the commercially produced pet foods specifically made for the purpose.

It is very important to watch your dog's weight as they get older. With less exercise weight gain could be a problem. Do not rely on weight charts to check your dog's weight but run your hands down the side over the ribs. You should be able to feel and count them. If you cannot, then your dog may be overweight and may need to go on a diet. Always seek professional advice before you cut back on your dog's food because they still need to be fed a balanced diet.

Certain breeds, such as the Pug, are prone to putting on excess weight and their diet must be monitored carefully

EXERCISE

As your pet ages they may well start to slow down. Some do so gradually, some do so suddenly and others, for example terriers, never seem to! Some of the changes you may notice are: they walk beside you rather than dashing to and fro; they are less keen to go on longer walks and they may

Fourteen-year-old Golden Retriever enjoying a swim

Regular exercise is essential

need a little help to get over that stile, they may also need a little help to get into the car at the end of a walk.

If your pet gets wet while out walking, dry them off as soon as possible, this is particularly important in cold weather. In snowy and icy conditions, check for snow or ice balls between their toes after walks.

A good example of a healthy thirteen-year-old Dalmatian

Unless medically contraindicated, older dogs should have routine regular exercise, with the emphasis on regular. Irregular bouts of strenuous exercise may give rise to stiff joints after a subsequent rest. Because they may be having less exercise, older dogs need to have their nails checked more regularly and trimmed appropriately.

Fourteen-year-old Golden Retriever at play

SPECIAL SENSES

All sensory organs can deteriorate with age, resulting in irreversible changes which can affect a dog's response to external stimuli.

HEARING

Partial or complete deafness is not uncommon in older dogs and may first be noticed by owners when their dog does not respond to commands or when calling them fails to rouse them from sleep. Although deafness may be caused by changes in the outer canal such as excess wax, growths or narrowing of the canal, most cases are due to changes beyond the eardrum. Although deafness can be a benefit in cases where dogs are frightened by fireworks, thunder or loud bangs, extra care must be taken with deaf patients as they have been deprived of one of their defence mechanisms. Some dogs that appear deaf may respond to a high-pitched frequency whistle, and watch out for those clever dogs which acquire selective hearing – the ones which ignore commands but can hear a sweet paper at a hundred paces.

EYESIGHT

There are many conditions that can affect dogs' eyes as they grow old. Certain breeds, e.g. Collies, Irish Setters, Cocker Spaniels and Miniature Poodles are subject to retinal degeneration and affected individuals may initially exhibit night blindness, which eventually progresses to blindness in bright light.

Cataracts, which appear as blue-white opacities of the lens are common in dogs over nine years of age. Although the opacity may be very obvious, the dog may retain reasonably good vision. Cataracts can be removed although the operation is more difficult in dogs than in humans.

Eyelid tumours are common in older dogs and appear as small swellings on the margin of the eyelids. They often have a large root below the surface and can bleed if rubbed. They are usually benign growths and can be removed surgically if they cause problems.

Cocker Spaniels are often prone to retinal degeneration

Cataracts can be seen clearly in all of these dogs

Discolouration of the surface of the eye is more common in some breeds than in others, for example it is often seen in German Shepherds, Cavalier King Charles Spaniels, Cocker Spaniels and Pekingese. The eye develops a brown cast across the surface and small blood vessels may be seen running across the eye. This is a condition that needs to be caught early to prevent chronic damage and impaired eyesight.

Conjunctivitis, which may be very acute in onset, can be caused by a number of factors including infections, irritants, trauma etc. On pulling the lower lid down the conjunctiva may be seen and in cases of conjunctivitus may appear very red and inflamed. The eye may have a yellow, white or green discharge. In severe cases, the white part of the eyeball may become involved.

Professional help should be sought when eye problems arise before irreversible changes take place.

Cavalier King Charles Spaniels often suffer from discolouration of the surface of the eye

Dogs with poor sight can still enjoy a good quality of life, and even totally blind dogs will learn to find their way around the home as long as furniture is left in the same place. Once outside on a lead blind dogs will learn to rely upon their owners to keep them out of trouble much in the same way that blind people trust their guide dogs.

Elderly dogs still enjoy exercise and play

TASTE

It is not thought that loss of taste is a common feature of ageing in dogs. Dogs may become more fussy as far as food is concerned as they grow older, but if a decrease in appetite is accompanied by weight loss, and/or other signs of ill-health, they should be checked by a veterinary surgeon as there may be some underlying disease causing the problem.

A healthy elderly Chow Chow. This breed has the distinction of having a black tongue and black gums

SMELL

As with taste, it is not believed that loss of smell is a significant problem with older dogs. Smell is the first sense to develop and, with most dogs, remains keen up until the end. You will see many dogs with failing eyesight relying heavily on their sense of smell to navigate their way around. Dogs with unusual nasal discharges, or with persistent sneezing episodes should be examined for problems involving the nose or mouth.

COMMON PROBLEMS

EXCESSIVE THIRST

With some pets an excessive thirst can be a normal physiological change, with others it can be a sign of disease. The most common causes of excessive thirst in older dogs are kidney failure, diabetes, liver problems, adrenal problems and, where a bitch has not been neutered, a septic womb.

If your pet develops a persistent excessive thirst you should seek veterinary attention. Taking a urine sample with you will help, but a blood sample may well be required to confirm a diagnosis.

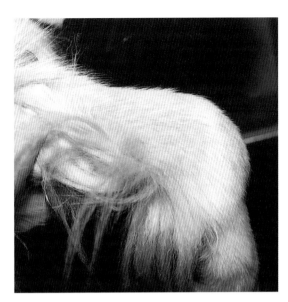

STIFF JOINTS

Many older, larger, heavier dogs suffer from joint problems. These problems are usually gradual in onset and changes may start well before the symptoms become obvious. Joints commonly affected are the hip, the stifle or knee, the elbow, the carpus or wrist and the lumbar spine or back.

Certain breeds are more prone to arthritic conditions than others. Generally speaking the larger and the heavier the dog, the more likely they are to suffer from degenerative joint disease or arthritis. The usual signs are stiffness and pain in one or more joints and these symptoms may be more pronounced when the patient first gets up, especially where a period of rest has been preceded by a period of strenuous exercise. The symptoms often improve with exercise, only to return after another period of inactivity.

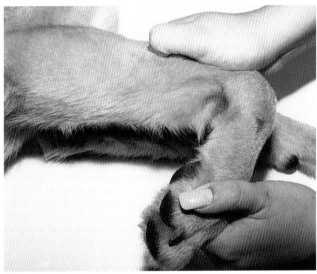

Arthritic joints are often swollen and painful if flexed or extended. The hair over the affected joint may be stained a rusty colour. This is because dogs often lick affected joints and saliva and tears turn an orange/rusty colour when exposed to the air

Affected joints may feel thickened when compared with the same joint on the other leg. There may be restricted movement or pain when the joint is manipulated. There may be crepitus or creaking, which can be felt, when the joint is flexed or extended.

In cases of back pain, affected dogs may be reluctant to go up steps, jump into the car or may appear stiff on both back legs.

Although it may not be possible to prevent degenerative joint disease, by keeping your dog's weight under control you should be able to delay the onset and/or minimise the changes.

WEAK BACK END

There is a reasonably common condition that affects certain breeds, such as German Shepherds, Collies, Labradors, Retrievers and their crosses, that can look like arthritis but is characterised by weakness rather than stiffness and pain.

This condition is called CDRM or Chronic Degenerative Radiculomyelopathy and it is more common in males than in females.

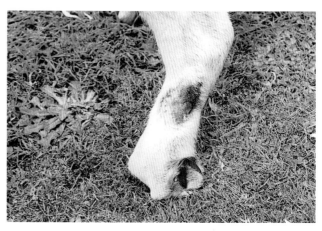

Knuckling over means that the foot is the wrong way round and this often leads to friction sores (*below*)

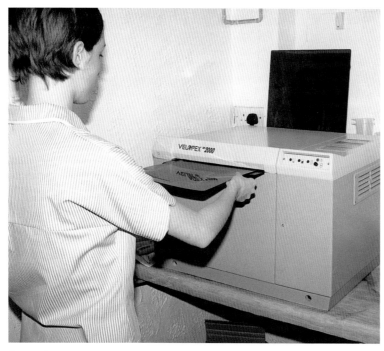

Processing an X-ray

The symptoms are slow in onset and only the back legs are affected. Knuckling and scuffing of the toes is a common complaint. Sometimes the back legs cross over and the dog may fall when turning a sharp corner. In advanced cases, patients may become incontinent.

It may prove necessary to X-ray a patient and carry out additional tests to establish the presence of arthritis or the extent of the problem before suitable treatment can be prescribed.

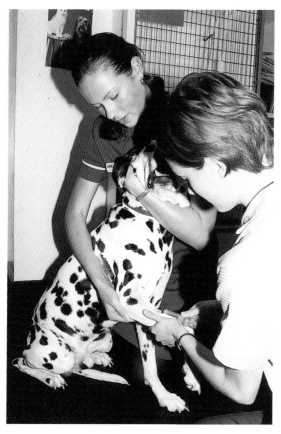
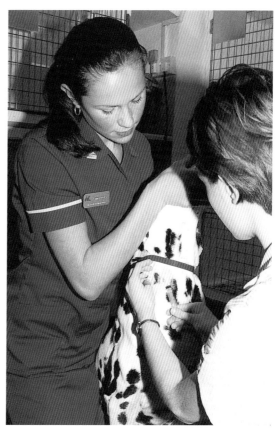

Taking a blood sample is a simple procedure and the result can reveal a great deal

URINARY PROBLEMS

Both male and female dogs can suffer from urinary problems as they grow older. Straining to pass urine is a symptom of a number of conditions, and is something that should be seen to as a matter of urgency.

Dogs suffering from cystitis will strain frequently to pass small amounts of urine and the urine may contain traces of blood. These may also be the symptoms of bladder stones, or prostate problems in male dogs. Male dogs that repeatedly strain to pass urine *without* success should receive urgent veterinary attention as they may have a blockage.

Bitches which have been neutered may develop urinary incontinence in old age. Owners may notice damp patches where

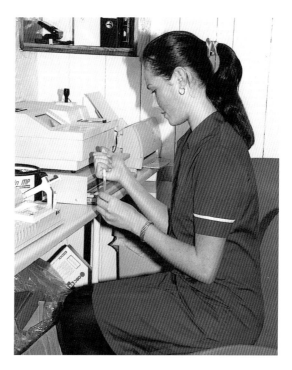

their pet has been asleep. This is because the urine simply leaks out when the dog is completely relaxed. Generally speaking dogs will soil their bed only as a last resort, and if this is happening your veterinary surgeon will probably be able to resolve the problem by giving you drops to add to your pet's food.

If you have to take your dog to the vet with a urinary problem, take a urine sample with you, along with details of just how much your pet is drinking each day. This may prove useful in helping to reach a diagnosis. Do not be alarmed if your veterinarian advises a blood test to help them reach a diagnosis.

Warts are harmless skin masses that protrude from the skin surface. They are usually multiple in number and can appear anywhere on the body, often on the face and limbs

LUMPS AND BUMPS

Many dogs will get lumps and bumps as they age. These masses vary from harmless warts and fatty lumps, through masses that are troublesome because of their position to tumours that are life-threatening.

Warts are usually small, irregular, pink or black cauliflower-like growths that protrude from the skin. They can occur anywhere over the body, and are commonly found on the face, head and legs. They may cause no problems whatsoever, but they can bleed or become infected. If they do, dogs will often lick at them persistently, making matters worse. Do not be tempted to put human wart medications on dogs as they are highly caustic.

Lipomas, or fatty lumps, are common in older dogs, especially if they are over-weight. They can occur anywhere over the body under the skin, but are most common over the trunk

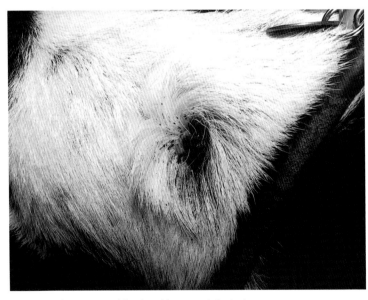

If damaged, warts can bleed and become infected

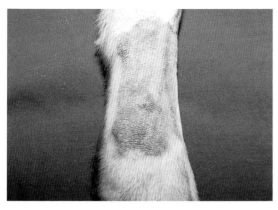 

Fibromas and other skin tumours are not uncommon in older dogs. Some are harmless but others are serious and all abnormal swellings should be checked

rather than on the head or legs. They are soft to the touch and usually moveable. In themselves they are harmless and slow growing, but they may be debilitating if they occur in an awkward position such as the armpit or groin.

Another reasonably common site for growths in older male dogs is just around the anus. These anal adenomas appear as small raised swellings which may bleed if disturbed. They are influenced by male hormones and your vet may recommend neutering your dog along with removing the growth to try to prevent further growths from developing.

If your dog has any swelling that should not be there, especially if it is growing rapidly, is bleeding or is painful to touch, have your veterinarian check it out. They may be able to make a diagnosis there and then or they may have to carry out some tests to see whether the mass should be removed.

MOUTH PROBLEMS

Enamel is the hardest substance in the body. If only gums were as tough! Like their owners, dogs lose more teeth due to gum disease than with problems associated with the teeth themselves. In fact cavities, which are very common in man, are very rare in dogs.

A dog's teeth should be white, and their gums pink. In time, without routine care, teeth develop a hard, yellowish grey substance on their surfaces called calculus.

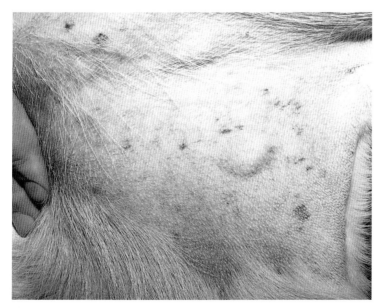

Lipomas are harmless fatty lumps that can appear anywhere under the skin but are usually found on the trunk and abdomen. They are soft, mobile and painless but can cause problems because of their location

Benson the Bulldog shows typical dental and gum changes that can come with old age

Check your dog's teeth on a regular basis, paying particular attention to where the tooth enters the gum. In particular, check the canines (fangs) and pull the lips back to reveal the large molars at the back of the mouth.

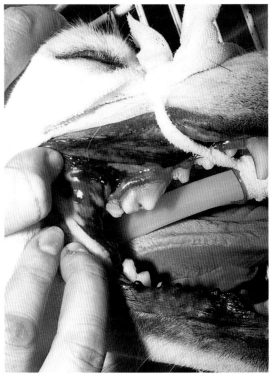

The calculus gradually gets between the tooth and the gum, allowing infection to set in and resulting in a breakdown of the ligament that holds the tooth in place. The process is accompanied by bad breath, inflamed and maybe even bleeding gums and varying degrees of discomfort and pain. Once a dog's teeth have reached this stage, they will need to be cleaned professionally, under a general anaesthetic. This usually involves ultrasonic scaling and polishing.

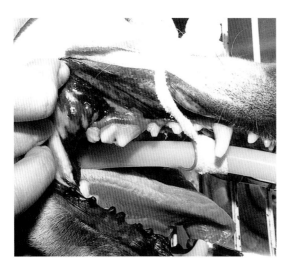

Plaque and calculus appears as grey, yellow staining on the teeth. It leads to inflammation of the gums, gum erosion and eventual loss of teeth

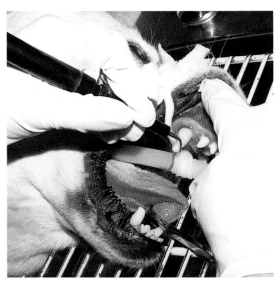

Teeth being ultrasonically scaled under anaesthetic

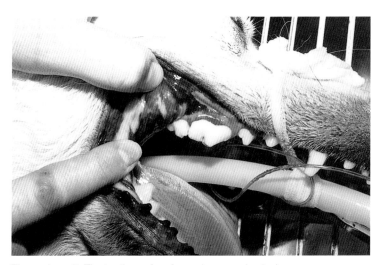

The end result. The teeth are free from plaque and calculus.
The endotracheal tube carries the anaesthetic gases to the patient

Infected mouths not only cause pain and localised problems, but can lead to general illness, including heart problems.

There are several things you can do to help keep your dog's teeth and gums in good condition. Daily brushing, with a doggy toothpaste, feeding them dry foods and encouraging them to chew all help to develop strong and healthy gums and sound teeth.

BEHAVIOUR

FITS

Fits or seizures are usually caused by abnormal neurological activity and the severity of the fit may vary from a very mild twitch to a full blown seizure. In mild cases the fit may be very transient, with the patient returning to normal in a matter of minutes. In severe cases one fit may lead into the next with little respite in between. In older patients there are many causes of fits and seizures and veterinary treatment should be sought if they occur. It is very unusual for a dog to swallow its own tongue during a fit or seizure and owners should be very wary of putting their fingers too near a fitting dog's mouth in case they get bitten by mistake.

Golden Retriever aged fourteen years

STROKES

Just like us, dogs can have strokes and, as in humans, they happen without warning. A dog can be perfectly normal one minute and in a confused, uncoordinated, distressed state the next. Sometimes a stroke is accompanied by vomiting, urination, defaecation or a fit. A stroke normally affects one side of the brain and patients will usually veer or fall to one side, have a head tilt and, if you look carefully at their eyes, they will be flicking rhythmically and uncontrollably from side to side.

If your dog has a fit, try to remain calm and try to comfort and support them. Try to restrain them to prevent them from crashing into objects and harming themselves and seek veterinary attention immediately.

Strokes can be minor to severe in nature, and many dogs make good recoveries, although it may well take a matter of weeks or months to do so. Treatment is aimed at relieving the acute symptoms and improving the circulation to the brain.

COLLAPSING EPISODES

Unlike a fitting dog, a collapsing dog will appear very weak and lethargic. Poor circulation is one of the most common causes of weakness in older dogs and to check the state of your dog's circulation, lift the upper lip and look at the colour of the gums.

Normal gums should look pink and should not be pale or bluish. (Some dogs' gums may have patches of black which is all right, and Chows have all-black gums.) Apply pressure to the gum with your finger for a couple of seconds, then release and observe. Normal gums should regain their colour within a couple of seconds.

This elderly Retriever shows signs of facial nerve damage with the tell-tale droopy eye

With most heart conditions the onset of symptoms is insidious, so should your dog collapse suddenly, the cause my lie elsewhere. A relatively common cause of sudden collapse, especially in large breeds (German Shepherds in particular) is internal haemorrhage from a tumour of the spleen. Again, the gums will look very pale and the dog's abdomen may look swollen. These tumours can rupture spontaneously and there may be no external trauma prior to onset. Any alteration in your dog's exercise tolerance should be investigated, and a sudden collapse should be treated as an emergency.

SENILITY

Just like people, dogs may grow old gracefully, retaining all their faculties in virtually full working order right up until the end. That is what we would all like for ourselves and for those around us but it doesn't always work out that way.

Signs of senility may include the inability to teach an old dog a new trick, and this is because mental alertness, memory and learning ability may all be impaired. Old dogs may show decreased alertness, poor reactions, and failure to recognise familiar surroundings or people. They may exhibit altered sleeping patterns and may be harder to wake from a deep sleep, often responding with a start when roused. They may forget their house training and start fouling indoors.

Some of these changes could be caused by specific medical problems, but they may simply be due to impaired functionality associated with ageing. Dogs exhibiting one or more of the symptoms detailed above may well benefit from a thorough clinical examination and perhaps a blood test to check their health.

An alteration in diet or specific medication may be beneficial in some cases. There are medicines available now that can improve the quality of life in cases where the older pet is simply, for want of a better term, slowing down. These work by improving the circulation to areas such as the brain, the muscles, the heart, the intestines and other areas, resulting in an improvement in some of the symptoms associated with senility.

Two elderly Pugs (*left*) aged twelve and (*right*) aged eleven

MEDICATION AND THE OLDER DOG

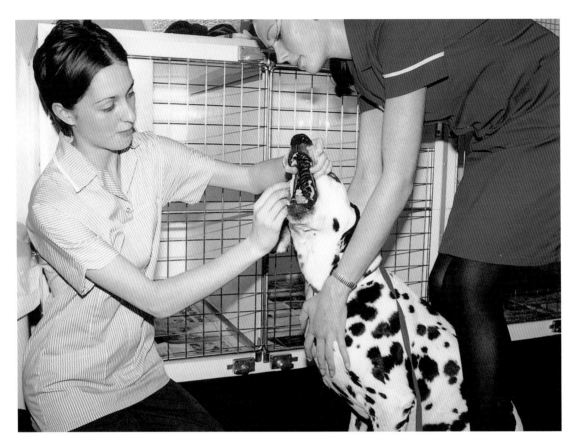

Because our pets are now living longer, they will often develop surgical or medical problems that need addressing.

The first stage in any treatment is making a diagnosis, and veterinarians rely heavily upon an owner's history of their pet's behaviour in helping them to make that diagnosis. What is it that their pet has stopped, or started, doing? When did the problem start? How much extra are they drinking? Is the lameness worse after resting? And so on. Bringing in a urine sample may well prove very useful. There then follows a detailed clinical examination. It may well prove necessary to take a blood sample to help reach a diagnosis. Many veterinary practices now have their own laboratories and results may be available the same day. Some samples may need to be sent away to external laboratories and it may take a few days to get the results.

Where tumours or growths are concerned, it may be possible to take a biopsy using a fine needle, under sedation or local anaesthetic. With more deep-seated masses a general anaesthetic may be required. An ECG, X-ray or ultrasound scan may be indicated in some cases.

Some veterinary practices now offer their clients a Senior Pet Programme, along the lines of a full health screen, where the patient is admitted for the day for a thorough examination and various medical tests.

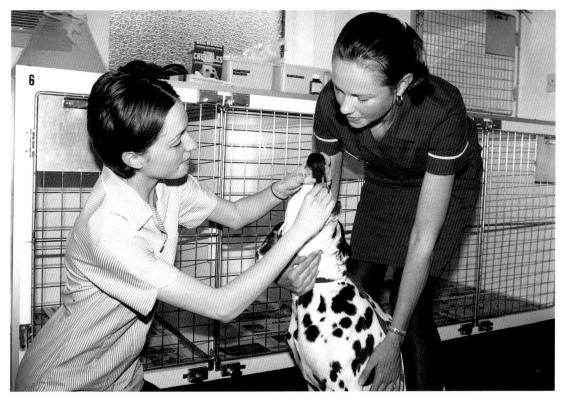

Giving a pill (*opposite and this page*)

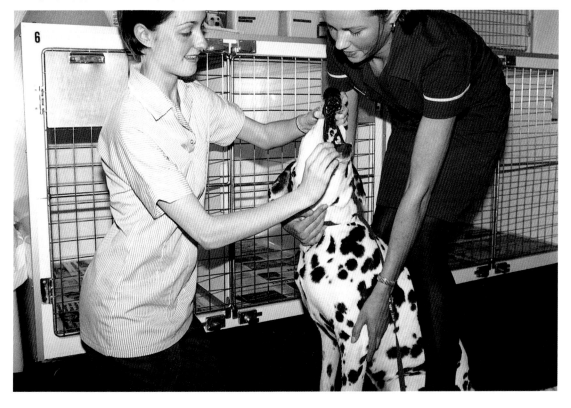

Having reached a diagnosis, treatment can be instituted. This may be something as simple as an alteration in diet, or it may involve a course of medical or surgical treatment. The medication may be for a limited period, or in cases of chronic illness such as heart problems or arthritis, may be permanent.

Some medications may have side effects and if this is a common feature, such as bowel upsets with certain anti-arthritis medications, your veterinarian will discuss these with you. Whatever medication your pet is on, you should report any adverse reactions to your vet.

INTRODUCING A NEW DOG

To many people their dog is their only companion and to be without one would be unthinkable. As a pet enters their latter years, many people ponder the difficult question as to whether they should obtain a canine companion for their ageing friend. The success or otherwise of this move depends very much upon the health and temperament of the existing pet and the temperament of the new one.

Whilst it can be a good idea to introduce a new puppy, this could be excessive!

Holly, a ten-year-old Cavalier King Charles Spaniel with young playmate Flora

Always put the needs of your existing pet above your own and those of the new dog. Remember that a new puppy is going to be very lively and will want to play rough. Will your existing pet appreciate the rough and tumble? A young, lively puppy may be the last thing an older infirm dog will appreciate. On the other hand, the introduction of a new companion may well give an older dog a new lease of life. Nobody will know your existing pet better than you. How do they get on with other dogs? Are they tolerant or have they become short-tempered with old age? Can you borrow a friend's dog to gauge their reaction to sharing the house with a pal?

Having obtained a new dog, make sure you introduce them gradually. Keep the new dog in a separate room for a few days.

The older pet will learn of their presence through sound and smell. Introduce them for short periods initially and always give more attention to the older pet. Make sure that the older pet is fed first and that well-established routines involving the older pet are adhered to.

If you do decide to get another dog, give it a great deal of thought beforehand.

WHEN IT IS TIME TO PART COMPANY

Death is the only real certainty in life and most of us, given the choice, would probably like to end our days at home surrounded by family members, drifting off to sleep, free from pain in our own beds. Naturally, this is also what most dog owners would like for their pets but unfortunately it is not what happens in the majority of cases. We say unfortunately, but taking positive action to help a much loved pet on that final journey is frequently the last favour we can do for them. When a pet is suffering from an incurable disease, or when the quality of life is such that it is unfair to carry on, a painless injection, which is nothing more than an anaesthetic overdose is often the kindest course of action.

Many dog owners put off taking their elderly ill pets to the veterinarian, in fear that they will be put to sleep, but the decision to end a pet's life will always be a joint one, made between the owner and the veterinarian. Many conditions that affect our older patients can be cured. In cases where the problem cannot be resolved, very often the symptoms can be alleviated and the sooner

a problem is addressed the greater the success level is likely to be. The veterinarian's role is to determine the pet's state of health, to make a diagnosis and to give a prognosis and the owner's role is to judge the dog's quality of life in the home environment.

As a dog ages and as problems arise, owners frequently ask how they will know when it is the correct time to make that final decision. Where a close bond exists between an owner and a pet, people seem to know instinctively when the time has come and their veterinarian will be in a position to confirm that decision or to offer an alternative course of action.

It is quite natural for owners to experience a raft of emotions on losing a pet, especially when they have had them put-to-sleep. Grief and loss certainly, and in many cases guilt. Guilt that they have let their pet down, remorse that they have prematurely ended their dog's life. Owners often find it beneficial to discuss the many questions surrounding euthanasia in advance of the euthanasia consultation with their veterinary practice.

ACKNOWLEDGEMENTS

The author is most grateful to the dog owners who have allowed photographs of their dogs to appear in this book. He is especially grateful to Hill's Pet Nutrition Ltd for their help in supplying photographs and to the staff and clients of Woodcroft Veterinary Group.

The photographs on pages 7, 10 (top), 17, and 19 courtesey of Animal Photography © Sally Anne Thompson, also page 5 (bottom) © R Willbie.

British Library Cataloguing-in-Publication Data.
A catalogue record for this book is available from the British Library

ISBN 0.85131.779.0

© Geoff Little 2000
Geoff Little asserts his right to be identified as the author of this work in accordance with the Copyright, Design and Patent Act 1988

No part of this book may be reproduced, stored in a retrieval system, or transmitted, in any form or by any means, electronic, mechanical, photocopying, recording or otherwise, without the prior permission of the publisher. All rights reserved.

Published in Great Britain in 2000 by
J. A. Allen an imprint of Robert Hale Ltd.,
Clerkenwell House, 45–47 Clerkenwell Green,
London EC1R 0HT

Series design by Paul Saunders, layout by Dick Vine
Series editor John Beaton
Colour processing by Tenon & Polert Colour Scanning Ltd., Hong Kong
Printed in Hong Kong by Dah Hua International Printing Press Co. Ltd.